Mel Bay presents

Great hymns for Guitar

By Bill Bay

The hymn settings collected in this master volume span centuries. I have selected hymns which convey the strength, power and victory of the Christian message. The hymns selected are sung frequently in all denominations and are timeless in their musical value and in the message which they convey. There also are a number of new settings included in this collection. All songs are arranged for a two-part vocal melody with guitar accompaniment to singing. The guitar accompaniment parts are written in notation and tablature. It is hoped that this master collection will be a valuable resource tool for any guitarist involved in Christian worship.

Bill Bay

PSALM 150:4

. . . . . . praise him with stringed instruments . . . . . .

CONTENTS

How to Read Tablature

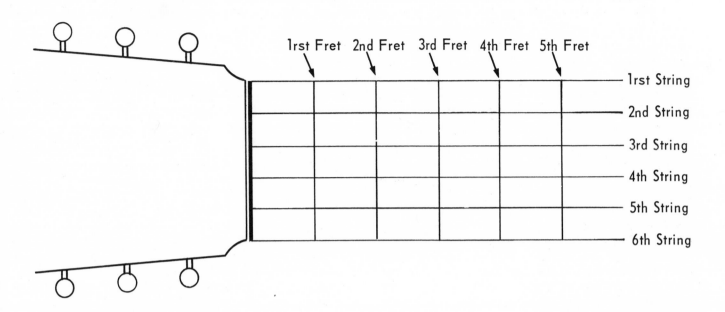

In Tablature the lines Represent Strings. The numbers appearing on the lines indicate Frets. (o = open string) In the following Example a C chord would be played. (1st String Open, 2nd String press Down on the 1st Fret, 3rd String Open, 4th String press down on the 2nd Fret, 5th String press down on the 3rd Fret, and Finally do not play the 6th String.)

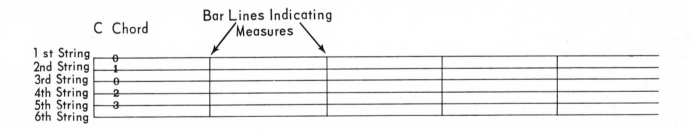

Rhythm in Tablature

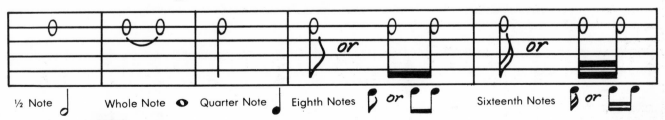

Bread Of The World

Reginald Heber
1783-1826

John S. B. Hodges
1830-1915

1. Bread of the world in mer - cy bro - ken,
2. Look on the world heart by sor - row bro - ken,

Wine of the soul in mer - cy shed,
Look on the soul tears by sin - ners shed,

By whom the words of life were spo - ken,
And by thy feast to us the to - ken

And in whose death our sins____ are dead!
that by Thy grace our souls____ are fed! A - men.

Here, O My Lord, I See Thee

Horatius Bonar
1808-1889

Edward Dearle
1806-1891

1. Here, O my Lord, I see Thee face to face; Here would I touch and handle things un-seen, Here grasp with firm-er hand e-ter-nal grace, And all my wea-ri-ness up-on Thee lean.

2. This is the hour of ban-quet and of song; This is the heav'n-ly ta-ble spread for me; Here let me feast, and feast-ing, still pro-long The hal-lowed hour of fel-low-ship with Thee.

3. Here would I feed up-on the bread of God, Here drink with Thee the roy-al wine of heav'n, Here would I lay a-side each earth-ly load, Here taste a-fresh the calm of sin for-given.

4. Feast af-ter feast thus comes and pas-es by, Yet, pass-ing, points to the glad feast a-bove, Giv-ing sweet fore-taste of the fes-tal joy, The Lamb's great bri-dal feast of bliss and love. A-men.

5

My Jesus, I Love Thee

William R. Featherstone
1842-1878

Adoniram J. Gordon
1836-1895

1. My Je - sus I love Thee, I know Thou art mine, For
2. I love Thee be - cause Thou hast first lov - ed me, And
3. I'll love Thee in life, I will love Thee in death, And
4. In man - sions of glo - ry and end - less de - light I'll

Thee all the fol - lies of sin I re - sign; My
pur - chased my par - don on Cal - va - ry's tree; I
praise Thee as long as Thou lend - est me breath; And
ev - er a - dore Thee in heav - en so bright; I'll

gra - cious Re - deem - er, my Sav - ior art Thou; If
love Thee for wear - ing the thorns on Thy brow; If
say when the death - dew lies cold on my brow, If
sing with the glit - ter - ing crown on my brow, If

ev - er I loved Thee, my Je - sus, 'tis now.____
ev - er I loved Thee, my Je - sus; 'tis now.____
ev - er I loved Thee, my Je - sus; 'tis now.____
ev - er I loved Thee, my Je - sus; 'tis now.____ A - men.

Beneath The Cross Of Jesus

Elizabeth C. Clephane
1830-1869

Frederick C. Maker
1844-1927

1. Be - neath the cross of Je — sus I fain would take my stand, The shad - ow of a might - y rock With - in a wea - ry land: A home with-in the wil - der - ness, A rest up - on the way, From the burn - ing of the noon-tide heat And the bur - den of the day.

2. Up - on that cross of Je — sus Mine eye at times can see The ver - y dy - ing form of One Who suf - fered there for me; And from my smit - ten heart with tears Two won - ders I con - fess, The won - ders of His glo-rious love And my un-wor-thi - ness.

3. I take, O Cross, thy shad - ow For my a - bid - ing place; I ask no oth - er sun-shine than The sun - shine of His face; Con - tent to let the world go by, To know no gain or loss, My sin - ful self my on - ly shame, My glo - ry at the cross. A - men.

7

The Lord's Prayer

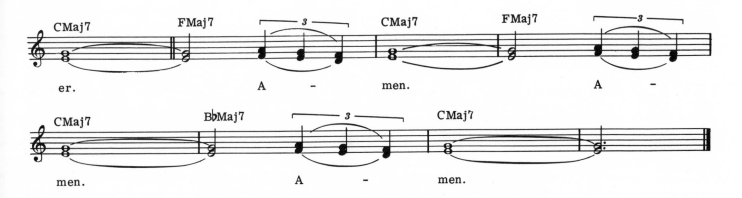

er.   A -   men.   A -

men.   A -   men.

Guitar Accompaniment

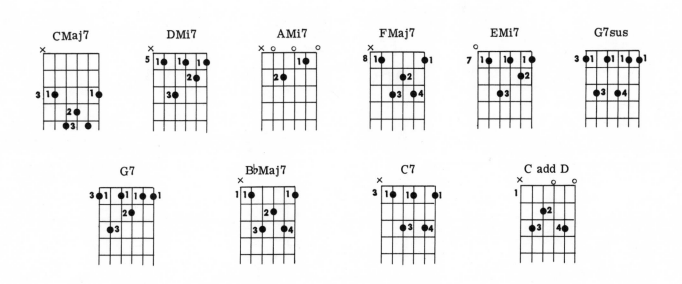

Be Known To Us In Breaking Bread

James Montgomery-1771-1854
Vs 2&3 Edward Osler
Vs. 1&4 (1836)

From
John Day's Psalter, 1562

1. O God, un-seen yet ev - er near, Thy pres - ence may we feel; And thus in-spired with ho - ly fear, Be-fore Thine al - tar kneel.
2. Be known to us in break-ing bread, But do not then de-part; Sav - ior, a - bide with us, and spread Thy ta - ble in our heart.
3. There sup with us in love di - vine; Thy bod - y and Thy blood, That liv - ing bread, that heav'n - ly wine, Be our im - mor - tal food.
4. Thus may we all Thy word o - bey, For we, O God, are Thine; And go re - joic - ing on our way: Re-newed with strength di - vine. A - men.

Jesus, The Very Thought Of Thee

John B. Dykes
1823-1876

1. Je - sus, the ver - y thought of Thee With sweet-ness
2. Nor voice can sing nor heart can frame, Nor can the
3. O Hope of ev - 'ry con - trite heart; O joy of
4. Je - sus, our on - ly joy be Thou, As Thou our

10

I Am Coming To The Cross

William McDonald
1820-1901

William G. Fischer
1835-1912

Something For Thee

Sylvanus D. Phelps
1816-1895

Robert Lowry
1826-1899

1. Sav - ior, Thy dy - ing love Thou gav - est me, Nor should I
2. Give me a faith - ful heart, Like - ness to Thee, That each de -
3. All that I am and have, Thy gifts so free, In joy, in

aught with-hold, Dear Lord, from Thee; In love my soul would bow,
part - ing day Hence forth may see Some work of love be - gun,
grief, thru life, Dear Lord, for Thee! And when Thy face I see,

My heart ful - fill its vow, Some of-f'ring bring Thee now, Some - thing for Thee.
Some deed of kind-ness done, Some wan-d'rer sought and won, Some - thing for Thee.
My ran-somed soul shall be, Thru all e - ter - ni - ty, Some - thing for Thee.

Lord, Speak To Me

Francis R. Havergal
(1836-1879)

Robert Schumann
1810-1856

1. Lord, speak to me, that I may speak In liv - ing ech - oes
2. O strength - en me, that while I stand Firm on the rock, and
3. O fill me with Thy ful - ness, Lord, Un - til my ver - y
4. O use me, Lord, use ev - en me Just as Thou wilt, and

All Praise To Thee, My God, This Night

Thomas Ken
(1637-1711)

This song may be sung as a round.

Thomas Tallis
c. 1520-1585

Glory Be To Jesus

Edward Caswall
Slowly

Friedrich Filitz
1847

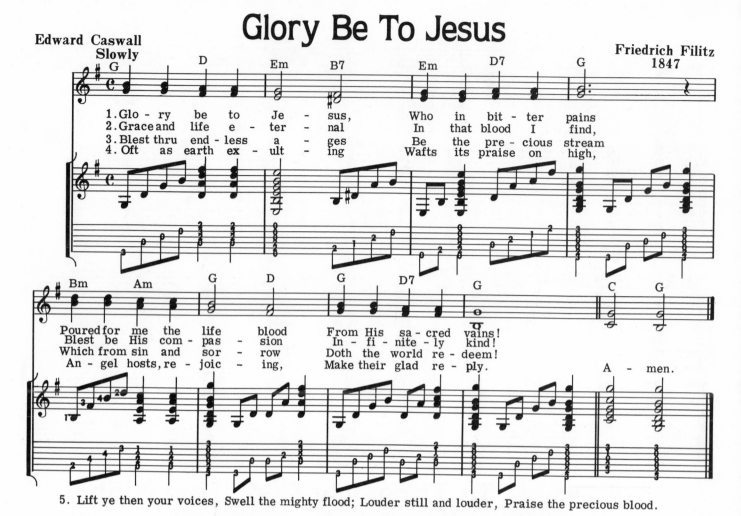

1. Glo - ry be to Je - sus, Who in bit - ter pains
2. Grace and life e - ter - nal In that blood I find,
3. Blest thru end - less a - ges Be the pre - cious stream
4. Oft as earth ex - ult - ing Wafts its praise on high,

Poured for me the life blood From His sa - cred vains!
Blest be His com - pas - sion In - fi - nite - ly kind!
Which from sin and sor - row Doth the world re - deem!
An - gel hosts, re - joic - ing, Make their glad re - ply. A - men.

5. Lift ye then your voices, Swell the mighty flood; Louder still and louder, Praise the precious blood.

O Come Let Us Adore Him

1. Oh come, let us a - dore Him, Oh come let us a - dore Him, Oh
2. We'll give Him all the glo - ry, We'll give Him all the glo - ry, We'll
3. For He a - lone is wor - thy, For He a - lone is wor - thy, For
4. We'll praise His name for - ev - er, We'll praise His name for - ev - er, We'll

come let us a - dore Him, Christ the Lord.
give Him all the glo - ry, Christ the Lord.
He a - lone is wor - thy, Christ the Lord.
praise His name for - ev - er, Christ the Lord.

Let All Mortal Flesh Keep Silence

17th Century
French Melody

1. Let all mor - tal flesh keep sil - ence, and with fear and
2. King of kings, yet born of Ma - ry, as of old on
3. At His feet the six - wing-ed ser - aph; cher - u - bim with

trem - bling stand; Pon - der noth - ing earth - ly mind - ed,
earth He stood, Lord of lords in hu - man ves - ture,
sleep - less eye, Veil their fac - es to the Pres - ence,

for with bless-ing in His hand. Christ our God to earth de -
in the Bo - dy and the Blood. He will give to all the
as with cease-less voice they cry, "Al - le - lu - ia, Al - le -

scend - eth, Our full hom-age to de - mand.
faith - ful His own self for heav - en - ly food.
lu - ia, Al - le - lu - ia, Lord most high. A - men.

Rejoice, Ye Pure In Heart

Edward H. Plumptre
1821-1891

Arthur H. Messiter
1834-1916

1. Re - joice, ye pure in heart, Re - joice, give thanks and sing; Your glo - ri - ous ban - ner wave on high, The cross of Christ your King.
2. Bright youth and snow crowned age, Strong men and mai - dens fair, Raise high your free, ex - ult - ing - song, God's won - drous praise de - clare.
3. Yes, on thru life's long path, Still chant - ing as ye go; From youth to age, by night and day, In glad - ness and in woe.
4. Still lift your stand - ard high, Still march in firm ar - ray, As war - riors thru the dark - ness toil Till dawns the gold - en day.

Refrain

Re - joice, re - joice, Re - joice, give thanks and sing. A - men.

Welcome, Happy Morning

Venantius Fortunatus c.530-609
Tr. by John Ellerton 1826-1893

Francis R. Havergal
1836-1879

1. "Wel-come, hap-py morn - ing," Age to age shall say; Hell to - day is van-quished,
2. Earth with joy con-fess - es, Cloth-ing her for spring, All good gifts re - turned with
3. Come then, true and faith - ful, Now ful-fill Thy word. 'Tis Thine own third morn-ing,

Heav'n is won to - day! Lo! the dead is liv - ing: God for ev - er - more,
Her re-turn-ing King, Bloom in ev-'ry mead - ow, Leaves on ev-'ry bough
Rise, O bur-ied Lord! Show Thy face in bright - ness, Bid the na-tions see,

Him, their true Cre - a - tor, All His works a - dore.
Speak His sor-rows end - ed, Hail His tri - umph now.
Bring a - gain our day-light: Day re-turns with Thee!

Refrain

"Wel-come, hap-py morn - ing,"

Age to age shall say; Hell to-day is van-guished, Heav'n is won to - day. A - men.

Come Christians, Join To Sing

Allegro
Christian Henry Bateman
1813-1889

Source Unknown

1. Come, Chris-tians, join to sing Al - le - lu - ia! A - men!
2. Come, lift your hearts on high; Al - le - lu - ia! A - men!
3. Praise yet the Lord a - gain; Al - le - lu - ia! A - men!

Lord praise to Christ our King; Al - le - lu - ia! A - men!
Let prais - es fill the sky; Al - le - lu - ia! A - men!
Life shall not end the strain; Al - le - lu - ia! A - men!

Let all, with heart and voice, Be - fore His throne re - joice;
He is our guide and friend; To us He'll con - des - cend,
On heav - en's bliss - ful shore His good - ness we'll a - dore,

Praise is His gra-cious choice: Al - le - lu - ia! A - men!
His love shall nev - er end: Al - le - lu - ia!
Sing - ing for - ev - er more Al - le - lu - ia! A - men.

18

When Morning Gilds The Skies

19th Century German Hymn
Trans. by Edward Caswall,
1814-1878

Joseph Barnby
1838-1896

1. When morn - ing gilds the skies_____ My heart a - wak - ing
2. Does sad - ness fill my mind?_____ A sol - ace here I
3. Ye na - tions of man - kind,_____ In this your con - cord
4. Be this, while life is mine,_____ My can - ti - cle di -

cries_____ May Je - sus Christ be praised: A -
find,_____ May Je - sus Christ be praised: Or____
find,_____ May Je - sus Christ be praised: Let____
vine,_____ May Je - sus Christ be praised: Be____

like at work and prayer_____ To Je - sus I re - pair; May
fades my earth - ly bliss?_____ My com - fort still is this, May
all the earth a - round_____ Ring joy - ous with the sound, May
this the 'e - ter - nal song_____ Thru all the a - ges long, May

Je - sus_____ Christ be_____ praised!
Je - sus_____ Christ be_____ praised!
Je - sus_____ Christ be_____ praised!
Je - sus_____ Christ be_____ praised! A - men.

To God Be The Glory

Fanny Crosby
1820-1915

William H. Doane
1832-1915

1. To God be the glo - ry, great things He hath done; So loved He the world that He gave us His Son, Who yield - ed His life an a - tone-ment for sin, And o - pened the life gate that all may go in.

2. O per - fect re - demp-tion, the pur - chase of blood, To ev - 'ry be - liev - er the prom-ise of God; The vil - est of-fend - er who tru - ly be - lieves, That mo - ment from Je - sus a par-don re - ceives.

3. Great things He hath taught us, great things He hath done, And great our re - joic - ing thru Je - sus the Son; But pur - er, and high - er, and great-er will be Our won-der, our trans-port, when Je - sus we see.

Refrain

Praise the Lord, praise the Lord, Let the earth hear His voice! Praise the Lord, praise the Lord, Let the peo - ple re -

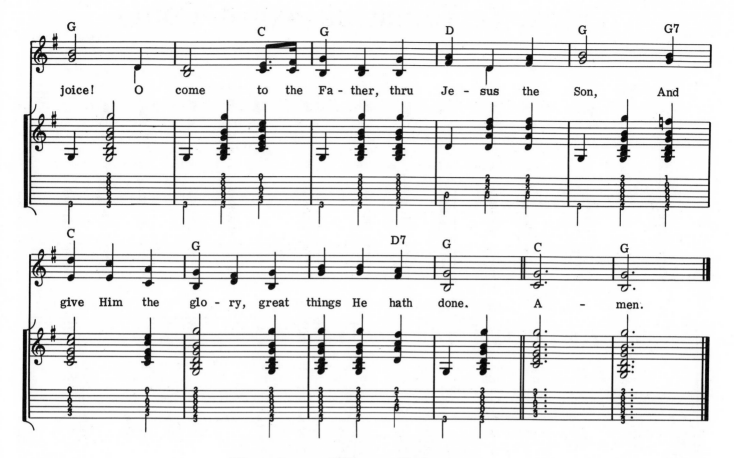

Praise The Savior

Thomas Kelly
1769-1854

German Melody

1. Praise the Sav-ior, ye who know Him! Who can tell how much we owe Him? Glad-ly
2. Je - sus is the name that charms us, He for con-flict fits and arms us; noth-ing
3. Trust in Him, ye saints for - ev - er He is faith-ful charg-ing nev - er! nei - ther

let us ren-der to Him All we are and have
moves and noth-ing harms us While we trust in Him.
force nor guile can sev - er Those He loves from Him. A - men.

Come, Ye Thankful People, Come

Henry Alford
1810-1871

George J. Elvey
1816-1893

1. Come, ye thank-ful peo - ple, come Raise the song of har - vest home:
2. All the world is God's own field, Fruit un - to His praise to yield:
3. For the Lord our God shall come And shall take His har - vest home:
4. E - ven so, Lord quick - ly come To Thy fi - nal har - vest home:

All is safe - ly geth - ered in Ere the win - ter storms be - gin.
Wheat and tares to - geth - er sown, Un - to joy or sor - row grown.
From His field shall in that day All of - fens - es purge a - way.
Gath - er Thou Thy peo - ple in, Free from sor - row, free from sin;

God, our Mak - er doth pro - vide For our wants to be sup - plied:
First the blade and then the ear, Then the full corn shall ap - pear:
Give His an - gels charge at last In the fire the tares to cast,
There, for-ev - er pu - ri - fied, In Thy pres - ence to a - bide:

Come to God's own tem - ple, come Raise the song of har - vest home.
Lord of har - vest, grant that we Whole some grain and pure may be.
But the fruit - ful ears to store In His gar - ner ev - er - more.
Come, with all Thine an - gels, come Raise the glo - rious har - vest home. A - men.

Crown His Head With Endless Blessing

W. Goode

William Moore in
"Columbian Harmony,"
1825

1. Crown His head with endless bless-ing, Who, in God the Fa-ther's name,
2. Lo, Je-ho-vah, we a-dore Thee; Thee, our Sav-ior! Thee our God!
3. Ho-ly, ho-ly, al-le-lu-ia! Heav'ns tri-umph-ant choir shall sing,

With com-pass-ions nev-er ceas-ing, Comes sal-va-tion to pro-claim.
From Your throne Your beams of glo-ry Shine through-out the world a-broad.
While the ran-somed na-tions fall be-fore the foot-stool of their King:

Hail, ye saints, who know His fav-or, Who with-in His gates are found;
In Your word Your light a-ris-es, Bright-est beams of truth and grace;
Then shall saints and ser-a-phim, Harps and voic-es, swell one hymn,

Hail, ye saints, our bless-ed Sav-ior, Let His courts with praise re-sound!
Bind, oh, bind our sac-ri-fi-ces, In Your courts our of-f'rings place.
Blend-ing in sub-lime ac-cord, sing-ing "Ho-ly, ho-ly, ho-ly Lord!"

Amazing Grace

John Newton
1725-1807

Early American Melody

5. Alleluia, Alleluia, Alleluia, Praise God! (Repeat)

Unto The Lamb We Sing Alleluia

John B. Dykes
1823-1876

W Bay, 1979

1. Un - to the Lamb we sing Al - le - lu - ia! Al - le - lu - ia! For Je-sus
2. Lord, fill us with Thy might - y Ho-ly Spir - it. Al - le - lu - ia! So we may

saves and heals and frees His peo - ple. Al - le - lu - ia!
Do the work for which you call us. Al - le - lu - ia!

Bend ev - 'ry knee and let all tongues con - fess
Be - fore Thy throne we hail Thee O Lord our King.

Je - sus is Lord, to Him sing Al - le - lu - ia!
Worth-y art Thou, our Sav - ior, Al - le - lu - ia! A - men.

Come Kingdom Of Our God

H. B. Johns

Wm A. Bay

1. Come, king - dom of our God, Sweet reign of light and love! Shed
2. Sweep o'er our spir - its first Ex - tend thy heal - ing reign; There
3. Come, king - dom of our God! And make the broad earth Thine; Stretch
4. Soon may all tribes be blest With fruit from life's glad tree; And

peace and hope and joy a - broad, And wis - dom from a - bove.
raise and quench the sa - cred thirst, That nev - er pains a - gain.
o'er her lands and isles the rod That flowers with grace di - vine.
in its shade like bro - thers rest, Sons of one fam - i - ly.

He Is Lord

1. He is Lord,
2. He's my Lord, He is Lord, He is ris - en from the dead and He is Lord, Ev - 'ry
3. You are Lord,

knee shall bow, Ev - 'ry tongue con - fess that Je - sus Christ is Lord.

Jesus Is His Name

Bill Bay

My God, How Great Thou Art

F.W.Faber From
"Spiritual Songs"

Adapt. From
Damon's Psalmes, 1579

1. My God, how great Thou art, Thy maj-es-ty how bright! How
2. I love Thee too, O Lord, Al-might-y as Thou art; For
3. No one can love like Thee, No moth-er half so mild For-
4. My God, how great Thou art, Thou ev-er-last-ing Friend! On

glo-rious is Thy mer-cy seat, In depths of burn-ing light!
Thou hast stooped to ask of me The love of my poor heart.
gives and loves as Thou hast done With me, Thy sin-ful child.
Thee I stay my trust-ing heart, Till faith in vis-ion end. A - men.

Come Sound His Praise Abroad

Isaac Watts

W. Bay

1. Come sound His praise a-broad, And hymns of glo-ry sing: Je-
2. He formed the deeps un-known; He gave the seas their bound: The
3. Come, wor-ship at His throne, Come, bow be-fore the Lord; We

ho-vah is the sov-reign God, The un-i-ver-sal King.
wat-ery worlds are all His own, And all the sol-id ground.
are His work and not our own, He formed us by His word.

O My Soul, Bless God The Father

From Paslm 103
United Presbyterian
of Psalms, 1871

Adapted From a Melody in
Psalmodia Sacra, 1715 by
Henry J. Gauntlett 1805-1876

1. O my soul, bless God the Fa - ther; All with - in me bless His name;
2. Who for - giv - eth thy trans - gres - sions, Thy dis - eas - es all who heals;
3. Bless the Fa - ther, all His crea - tures, Ev - er un - der His con - trol,

Bless the Fa - ther, and for - get not All His mer - cies to pro - claim.
Who re - deems thee from de - struction, Who with thee so kind - ly deals.
All through-out His vast do - min - ion: Bless the Fa - ther, O my soul A - men.

Bless The Lord, O My Soul

Source Unknown

Psalm 103:1

Bless the Lord, O my soul. Bless the Lord, O my soul And

all that is with - in me Bless His ho - ly name! A - men.

29

Fairest, Lord Jesus

From Münster Gesangbuch, 1677

From Schlesisch
Volkslieder, 1842
Adapted by Richard S. Willis
1819-1900

1. Fair - est Lord Je - sus, Ru - ler of al na - ture,
2. Fair are the mea - dows, Fair - er still the wood - lands,
3. Fair is the sun - shine, Fair - er still the moon - light,

O Thou of God and man the Son; Thee will I
Robed in the bloom - ing garb of spring: Je - sus is
And all the twink - ling, star - ry host: Je - sus shines

cher - ish, Thee will I hon - or, Thou, my soul's glo - ry,
fair - er, Je - sus is pur - er, Who makes the woe - ful
bright - er, Je - sus shines pur - er, Than all the an - gels

joy, and crown.
heart to sing.
heav'n can boast. A - men.

Holy, Holy, Holy

John B. Dykes
1823-1876

O For A Thousand Tongues To Sing

Charles Wesley
1707-1788

For Lower Key Play Chords in Parenthesis
E7(D7) A(G) E(D) D(C)

Carl Gläser
1784-1829

4. He breaks the pow'r of canceled sin,
   He sets the prisoner free;
   His blood can make the foulest clean;
   His blood availed for me.

5. He speaks, and listening to his voice,
   New life the dead receive;
   The mournful, broken hearts rejoice;
   The humble poor, believe.

6. Hear him, ye deaf; his praise, ye dumb,
   Your loosened tongues employ;
   Ye blind, behold your Savior come;
   And leap, ye lame, for joy.

Christ Be Beside Me

St. Patrick

Gaelic Melody

Crown Him With Many Crowns

Matthew Bridges
1823-1903

George J. Elvey
1816-1893

1. Crown Him with ma - ny crowns, The Lamb up - on His throne; Hark! how the heav'n - ly an - them drowns All mu - sic but its own: A - wake, my soul, and sing Of Him who died for thee, And hail Him as thy match-less King Through all e - ter - ni - ty.

2. Crown Him the Son of God Be - fore the worlds be - gan, And ye, who tread where He hath trod, Crown Him the Son of man; Who ev - 'ry grief hath known That wrings the hu - man breast, And takes and bears them for His own, That all in Him may rest.

3. Crown Him the Lord of life, Who tri - umphed o'er the grave, And rose vic - to - rious in the strife For those He came to save; His glo - ries now we sing Who died and rose on high, Who died, e - ter - nal life to bring, And lives that death may die.

4. Crown Him the Lord of lords, Who o'er the word doth reign, Who once on earth, the (in) car - nate Word, For ran - somed sin - ners slain, Now lives in realms of light, Where saints with an - gels sing Their songs be - fore Him day and night, Their God, Re - deem - er, King. A - men.

God The Omnipotent

Henry F. Chorley, 1808-1872
John Ellerion 1826-1893

Alevis Lvov
1798-1870

1. God the Om - nip - o - tent! King, who or - dain - est
2. God the All mer - ci - ful! earth hath for - sak - en
3. God the All right - eous One! man hath de - filed Thee;

Thun - der Thy clar - ion, the light - ning Thy sword;
Meek - ness and mer - cy, and slight - ed Thy word;
Yet to e - ter - ni - ty stand - eth Thy word;

Show forth Thy pit - y on high where Thou reign - est;
Let not Thy wrath in its ter - ors a - wak - en;
False - hood and wrong shall not tar - ry be - side Thee;

Give to us peace in our time, O Lord.
Give to us peace in our time, O Lord
Give to us peace in our time, O Lord A - men.

All Glory, Laud And Honor

Theodulph of Orleans, 760-821
Trans. John M. Neale 1818-1866

Melchior Teachner
1584-1635

1. All glo - ry, laud, and hon - or To Thee, Re - deem - er, King, To
2. The com - pa - ny of an - gels Are prais - ing Thee on high, And
3. To Thee, be - fore Thy pas - sion They sang their hymns of praise; To

whom the lips of chil - dren Made sweet ho - san - nas ring. Thou
mor - tal men and all things Cre - a - ted make re - ply. The
Thee, now high ex - alt - ed, Our mel - o - dy we raise. Thou

art the King of Is - ra - el, Thou Da - vid's roy - al Son, Who
peo - ple of the He - brews With palms be - fore Thee went; Our
didst ac - cept their prais - es; Ac - cept the prayers we bring, Who

in the Lord's name com - est, The King and bless - ed One.
praise and prayer and an - thems Be - fore Thee we pre - sent.
in all good de - light - est, Thou good and gra - cious King. A - men.

Holy God, We Praise Thy Name

Te Deum, c. 4th Century Attr.
To Ignaz Franz, 1719-1790
Trans. by Clarence Walworth, 1820-1900

From
"Katholisches Gesangbuch"
Vienna, c. 1774

1. Ho - ly God we praise Thy name; Lord of all we
2. Hark, the glad ce - les - tial hymn, An - gel choirs a -
3. Ho - ly Fa - ther, Ho - ly Son, Ho - ly Spir - it:

bow be - fore Thee; All on earth Thy scep - ter claim,
bove are rais - ing; Cher - u - bim and Ser - a - phim,
Three we name Thee; Though in es - sence on - ly One;

All in hea - ven a - bove a dore Thee; In - fi - nite Thy
In un - ceas - ing chor - us prais - ing, Fill the heav - ens with
Un - di - vid - ed God we claim Thee, And a - dor - ing

vast do - main, Ev - er last - ing is Thy reign.
sweet ac - cord; Ho - ly, ho - ly, ho - ly Lord.
bend the knee While we own the mys - te - ry. A - men.

Immortal, Invisible

Walter Chalmers Smith
1824-1908

Welsh Melody

1. Im - mor - tal, in - vis - i - ble, God on - ly wise, In
2. Un - rest - ing, un - hast - ing, and si - lent as light, Nor
3. To all, life Thou giv - est to both great and small, In
4. Great Fa - ther of glo - ry, pure Fa - ther of light, Thine

light in ac - ces - si - ble hid from our eyes, Most bless - ed, most
want - ing, nor wast - ing, Thou rul - est in might; Thy jus - tice, like
all life Thou liv - est the true life of all; All praise we would
an - gels a - dore Thee, all veil - ing their sight; All praise we would

glo - rious, the An - cient of Days, Al - might - y, vic -
moun - tains, high soar - ing a - bove tree, Thy clouds, which are
flour - ish as leaves on the tree, And with - er and
ren - der O help us to see 'Tis on - ly the

to - rious Thy great name we praise.
foun - tains of good - ness and love.
per - ish but naught chang - eth Thee.
splen - dor of light hid - eth Thee! A - men.

37

Now Thank We All Our God

Martin Rinkart
1586-1649
Trans Catherine
Winkworth 1827-1878

Johann Crueger, 1647

Boldly

1. Now thank we all our God, With heart, and hands, and voic - es, Who
2. O may this boun - teous God Through all our life be near us, With
3. All praise and thanks to God The Fa - ther now - be giv - en, The

won-drous things hath done, In whom His world re - joic - es; Who
ev - er joy - ful hearts And bless - ed peace to cheer us; And
Son, and Him who reigns With them in high - est heav - en, The

from our moth-er's arms Hath blessed us on our way With
keep us in His grace, And guide us when per - plexed, And
one e - ter - nal God, Whom earth and heav'n a - dore; For

count less gifts of love, And still is ours to - day.
free us from all ills In this world and the next.
thus it was, is now, And shall be ev - er - more. A - men.

38

O Worship The King

Robert Grant
1779-1838

J. Michael Haydn
1737-1806

1. O wor - ship the King, all glo - rious a - bove, And
2. O tell of His might, O sing of His grace, Whose
3. Thy boun - ti - ful care what tongue can re - cite? It
4. Frail chil - dren of dust, and fee - ble as frail, In

grate - ful - ly sing, His pow'r and His love; Our
robe is the light, whose can - o - py space; His
breathes in the air, it shines in the light; It
Thee do we trust, nor find Thee to fail; Thy

Shield and De - fend - er, the An - cient of Days, Pa -
char - iots of wrath the deep thun - der clouds form, And
streams from the hills, it de - scends to the plain And
mer - cies how ten - der! how firm to the end! Our

vil - ioned in splen-dor and gird - ed with praise.
dark is His path on the wings of the storm.
sweet - ly dis - tills in the dew and the rain.
Mak - er, De - fend - er, Re - deem - er and Friend. A - men.

39

All Hail The Power Of Jesus' Name

Edward Perronet
1726-1792

Oliver Holden
1765-1844

1. All hail the pow'r of Je-sus' name! Let an-gels pros-trate fall; Bring forth the roy-al di-a-dem, And crown Him Lord of____ all; Bring forth the roy-al di-a-dem, And crown Him Lord____ of all!____
2. Ye cho-sen seed of Is-rael's race, Ye ran-somed from the fall; Hail Him who saves you by__ His__ grace, And crown Him Lord of____ all; Hail Him who saves you by__ His__ grace, And crown Him Lord____ of all!____
3. Let ev-'ry kin-dred, ev-'ry tribe, On this ter-res-trial ball To Him all maj-es-ty__ as-cribe, And crown Him Lord of____ all; To Him all maj-es-ty__ as-cribe, And crown Him Lord____ of all!____
4. O that with yon-der sa-cred throng We at his feet may fall! We'll join the ev-er-last-ing__ song, And crown Him Lord of____ all; We'll join the ev-er-last-ing__ song, And crown Him Lord____ of all!____ A - men.

Praise To The Lord, The Almighty

Joachim Neander
1650-1680

Stralsund Gesangbuch
1665

1. Praise to the Lord, the Al - might-y, the King of cre - a - tion!
2. Praise to the Lord, who o'er all things so won-drous-ly reign - eth,
3. Praise to the Lord, who doth pros-per thy work and de - fend thee;
4. Praise to the Lord, O let all that is in me a - dore Him!

O my soul, praise Him for He is thy health and sal - va - tion!
Shield-eth thee un - der His wings, yea, so gent - ly sus - tain - eth!
Sure - ly His good - ness and mer - cy here dai - ly at - tend thee.
All that hath life and breath, come now with prais - es be - fore Him!

All ye who hear, Now to His tem - ple draw near;
Hast thou not seen How thy de - sires e'er have been
Pon - der a - new What the Al - might - y can do,
Let the a - men Sound from His peo - ple a - gain;

Join me in glad ad - o - ra - tion!
Grant - ed in what He or - dain - eth?
If with His love he be - friend thee.
Glad - ly for - ev - er a - dore Him. A - men.

The God of Abraham Praise

Based on the Yigdal
of Daniel ben Judah, ca 1400

Hebrew Melody
Arr. by Meyer Lyon
1751-1797

1. The God of A-braham praise, Who reigns en-throned a - bove; An-cient of ev - er - last - ing days, And God of love; To Him up-lift your voice, At___ whose su-preme com-mand___ From earth we rise, and seek the joys At___ His right hand.

2. He by Him-self hath sworn: I on His oath de-pend; I shall, on ea-gle wings up-borne, To heav'n as - cend: I shall be-hold His face, I___ shall His power a - dore,___ And sing the won-ders of His grace For___ ev - er - more.

3. There dwells the Lord, our King, The Lord, our Right-eous-ness, Tri-umph-ant o'er the world and sin, The Prince of Peace: On Zi - on's sa - cred height, His___ king-dom He main-tains,___ And glo-rious with His saints in light, For___ ev - er - more.

4. The God who reigns on high The great arch-an - gels sing, And "Ho - ly, Ho - ly, Ho - ly," cry Al - might - y King! Who was, and is, the same, And___ ev - er-more shall be:___ E - ter-nal Fa - ther, great I___ am, We___ wor - ship Thee." A - men.

42

For The Beauty Of The Earth

Folliott S. Pierpoint
1835-1917

Conrad Kocher
1786-1872

1. For the beau - ty of the earth, For the glo - ry of the skies, For the love which from our birth O - ver and a - round us lies: Lord of all, to Thee we raise This our hymn of grate - ful praise. A - men.

2. For the beau - ty of each hour Of the day and of the night, Hill and vale, and tree and flow'r, Sun and moon, and stars of light:

3. For the joy of hu - man love, Bro - ther, sis - ter, par - ent, child, Friends on earth, and friends a - bove; For all gen - tle thoughts and mild:

4. For thy church, that ev - er - more Lift - eth ho - ly hands a - bove, Of - f'ring up - on ev - 'ry shore Her pure sac - ri - fice of love:

I Will Praise Him

Margaret J. Harris
19th Cent.

1. When I saw the cleans-ing foun-tain O - pen wide for all my sin,
2. Then God's fire up-on the al - tar Of my heart was set a - flame;
3. Glo - ry, glo - ry to the Fa-ther! Glo - ry, glo - ry to the Son!

I o - beyed the Spir - it's woo - ing, When He said, "Wilt thou be clean?"
I shall nev - er cease to praise Him, Glo - ry, glo - ry to His name!
Glo - ry, glo - ry to the Spir - it! Glo - ry to the Three in One!

Chorus

I will praise Him! I will praise Him! Praise the Lamb for sin-ners slain:

Give Him glo-ry, all ye peo - ple, For His blood can wash a-way each stain.

44

Behold The Glories Of The Lamb

Verses Isaac Watts
Chorus Wm. Bay

Wm. Bay

1. Be-hold the glo-ries of the Lamb, A-mid His Fa-ther's throne; Pre-pare new hon-ors for His name, And songs be-fore un-known.
2. Let el-ders wor-ship at His feet, The chruch a-dore a-round, With vi-als full of o-dors sweet, And harps of sweet-er sound.
3. Now to the Lamb that once was slain, Be end-less bless-ings paid! Sal-va-tion, glo-ry, joy re-main For-ev-er on Thy head.
4. Thou hast re-deemed our souls with blood, Hast set the pri-soners free; Hast made us kings and priests to God, And we shall reign with Thee.

Chorus

Em-man - u - el, We lift up our hearts and we sing, Em-man - u - el, Our Lord, our Re-deem-er, and King!

Come, Ye That Love The Lord

Isaac Watts
1674-1748

Aaron Williams
1731-1776

1. Come, we that love the Lord, And let our joys be known; Join in a song with sweet ac-cord And thus sur-round the throne.
2. Let those re-fuse to sing Who nev-er knew our God; But chil-dren of the heav'n-ly King May speak their joys a-broad.
3. The hill of Zi-on yields A thou-sand sa-cred sweets Be-fore we reach the heav'n-ly fields Or walk the gol-den streets.
4. Then let our songs a-bound And ev-'ry tear be dry; We're march-ing thru Em-man-uel's ground To fair-er worlds on high. A - men.

Great God, When I Approach Thy Throne

Supplement to Kentucky
Harmony, 1820

1. Great God, when I ap-proach Thy throne, And all Thy glo-ry see; This
2. A-wake, my heart, a-rise, my tongue, Pre-pare a thank-ful voice; In
3. And Lord, when I be-hold Thy face, This must be all my plea; "Praise

46

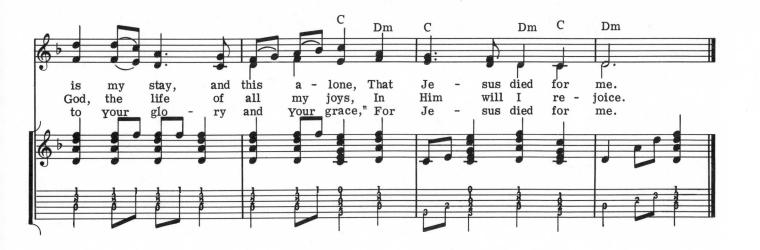

is my stay, and this a - lone, That Je - sus died for me.
God, the life of all my joys, In Him will I re - joice.
to your glo - ry and Your grace," For Je - sus died for me.

Allelu, Praise The Lord

By Bill Bay

Al - le - lu - ia, We thank you Lord, We mag - ni -

fy Your name. Our hearts spring forth with a

new song to You. Al - le - lu, Praise the Lord!

Glorious Things Of Thee Are Spoken

John Newton
1725-1807

Franz J. Haydn
1732-1809

1. Glo-rious things of Thee are spo-ken, Zi-on cit-y of our God;
2. See, the streams of liv-ing wa-ters, Spring-ing from e-ter-nal love,
3. Round each hab-i-ta-tion hov-'ring, See the cloud and fire ap-pear

He, whose word can not be bro-ken, Formed Thee for His own a-bode:
Well sup-ply Thy sons and daugh-ters, And all fear of want re-move:
For a glo-ry and a cov-'ring, Show-ing that the Lord is near!

On the Rock of A-ges found-ed, What can shake Thy sure re-pose?
Who can faint, while such a riv-er Ev-er flows their thirst t'as-suage?
Glo-rious things of Thee are spo-ken, Zi-on cit-y of our God;

With sal-va-tion's walls sur-round-ed Thou may'st smile at all Thy foes.
Grace which, like the Lord the giv-er, Nev-er fails from age to age.
He, whose word can-not be bro-ken, Formed Thee for His own a-bode. A-men.

O Day Of Rest And Gladness

Christopher Wordsworth
1807-1885

Old German
Melody

49

Come, Thou Almighty King

Felice De Giardini
1716-1796

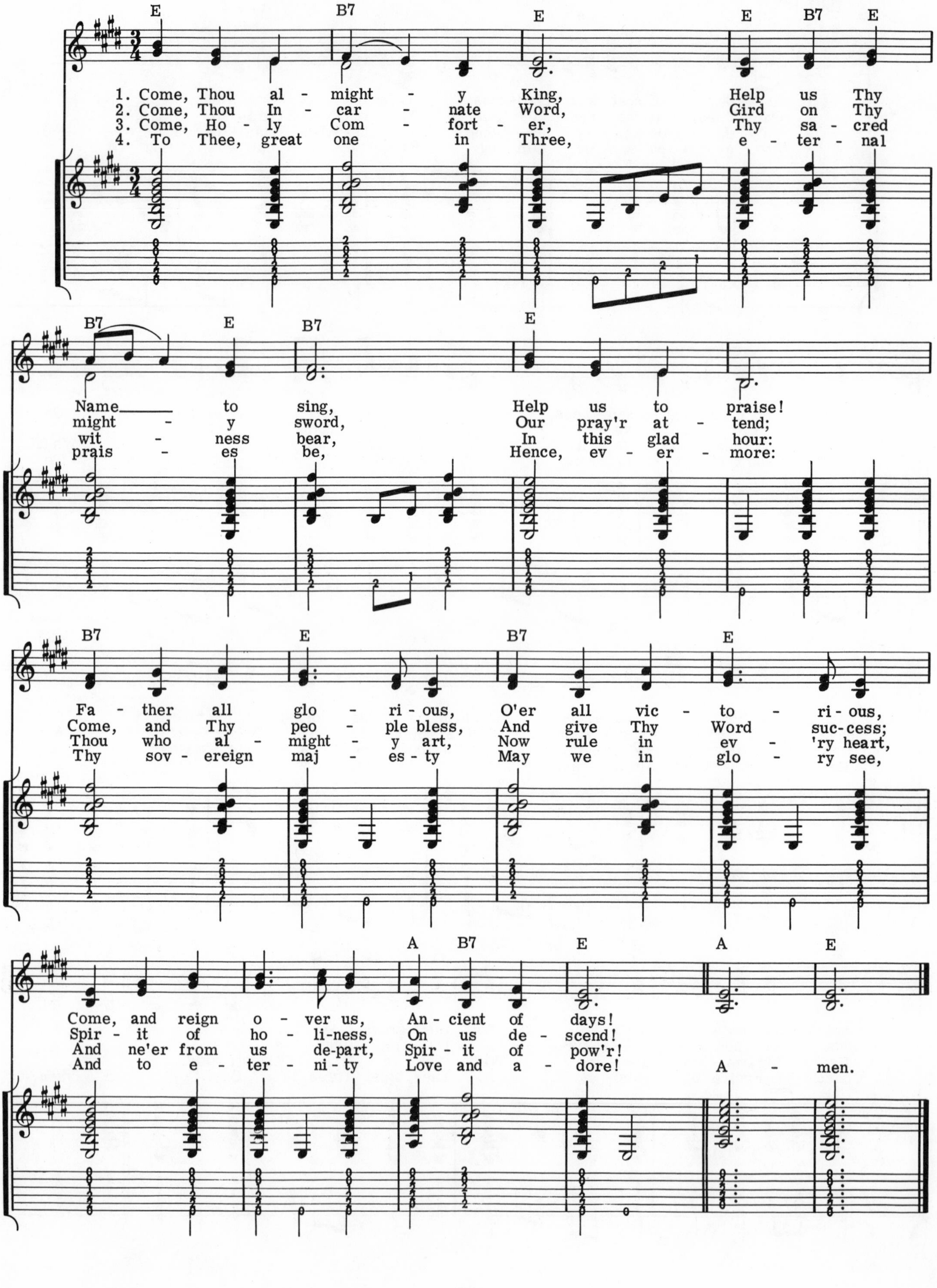

E B7 E E B7 E
1. Come, Thou al - might - y King, Help us Thy
2. Come, Thou In - car - nate Word, Gird on Thy
3. Come, Ho - ly Com - fort - er, Thy sa - cred
4. To Thee, great one in Three, e - ter - nal
B7 E B7 E
Name to sing, Help us to praise!
might - y sword, Our pray'r at - tend;
wit - ness bear, In this glad hour:
prais - es be, Hence, ev - er - more:
B7 E B7 E
Fa - ther all glo - ri - ous, O'er all vic - to - ri - ous,
Come, and Thy peo - ple bless, And give Thy Word suc - cess;
Thou who al - might - y art, Now rule in ev - 'ry heart,
Thy sov - ereign maj - es - ty May we in glo - ry see,
A B7 E A E
Come, and reign o - ver us, An - cient of days!
Spir - it of ho - li - ness, On us de - scend!
And ne'er from us de - part, Spir - it of pow'r!
And to e - ter - ni - ty Love and a - dore! A - men.

Mine Eyes And My Desire

51

When I Survey The Wondrous Cross

Isaac Watts
1674-1748

From A Gregorian
Chant

1. When I sur - vey the won - drous cross
2. For - bid it Lord, that I should boast,
3. See, from His head, His hands, His feet,
4. Were the whole realm of na - ture mine

On which the Prince of Glo - ry died,
Save in the death of Christ, my God;
Sor - row and love flow min - gled down;
That were an of - f'ring far too small;

My rich - est gain I count but loss,
All the vain things that charm me most,
Did e'er such love and sor - row meet,
Love so a - maz - ing, so di - vine,

And pour con - tempt on all my pride
I sac - ri - fice them to His blood.
Or thorns com - pose so rich a crown?
De - mands my soul, my life my all. A - men.

Love Divine

Charles Wesley
1707-1788

John Zundel
1815-1882

1. Love di - vine, all loves ex - cel - ling, Joy of heav'n to earth come down;
2. Breathe, O breathe Thy lov - ing Spir - it In - to ev - 'ry trou - bled breast!
3. Come al - might - y to de - liv - er, Let us all Thy life re - ceive;
4. Fin - ish then Thy new cre - a - tion, Pure and spot - less let us be;

Fix in us Thy hum - ble dwell - ing, All Thy faith - ful mer - cies crown.
Let us all in Thee in - her - it, Let us find that sec - ond rest.
Sud - den - ly re - turn and nev - er, Nev - er - more Thy tem - ples leave.
Let us see Thy great sal - va - tion Per - fect - ly re - stored in Thee.

Je - sus, Thou art all com - pas - sion, Pure, un - bounded love Thou art;
Take a - way our want for sin - ning, Al - pha and O - me - ga be;
Thee we would be al - ways bless - ing, Serve Thee as Thy hosts a - bove,
Changed from glo - ry in - to glo - ry, Till in heav'n we take our place,

Vis - it us with Thy sal - va - tion, En - ter ev - 'ry trem - bling heart.
End of faith, as its be - gin - ning, Set our hearts at li - ber - ty.
Pray and praise Thee with out ceas - ing, Glo - ry in Thy per - fect love.
Till we cast our crowns be - fore Thee, Lost in won - der, love and praise. A - men.

When I Can Read My Title Clear

Isaac Watts
1674-1748

Joseph C. Lowry
1820-?

Savior, Like A Shepherd Lead Us

From Dorothy Thrupp's
"Hymns for the Young" 1836

William B. Bradbury
1816-1868

1. Sav-ior like a shep-herd lead us, Much we need Thy ten-der care;
2. Thou hast prom-ised to re-ceive us, Poor and sin-ful tho' we be;
3. Ear-ly let us seek Thy fa-vor, Ear-ly let us do Thy will;

In Thy pleas-ant pas-tures feed us, For our use Thy folds pre-pare: Bless-ed
Thou hast mer-cy to re-lieve us, Grace to cleanse and pow'r to free: Bless-ed
Bless-ed Lord and on-ly Sav-ior, With Thy love our hearts fill: Bless-ed

Je-sus, Bless-ed Je-sus, Thou hast bought us, Thine we are; Bless-ed
Je-sus, Bless-ed Je-sus, Ear-ly let us turn to Thee; Bless-ed
Je-sus, Bless-ed Je-sus, Thou hast loved us, Love us still, Bless-ed

Je-sus, Bless-ed Je-sus, Thou hast bought us, Thine we are.
Je-sus, Bless-ed Je-sus, Ear-ly let us turn to Thee.
Je-sus, Bless-ed Je-sus, Thou hast loved us, love us still.

Just As I Am

Charlotte Elliott
1789-1871

Wm Bradbury
1816-1868

1. Just as I am, with-out one plea, But that Thy blood was
2. Just as I am, and wait-ing not To rid my soul of
3. Just as I am, tho tossed a-bout With man-y con - flict,
4. Just as I am, Thou wilt re-ceive, Wilt wel-come, par - don,

shed for me, And that Thou bidd'st me come to Thee
one dark blot, To Thee whose blood can cleanse each spot
many a doubt, Fight-ings and fears with - in, O
cleanse, re-lieve, Be - cause Thy prom - ise I be - lieve,

Lamb of God, I come! I

come! A - men.

Take Time To Be Holy

William D. Longstaff
1822-1894

George C. Stebbins
1846-1945

1. Take time to be ho - ly, Speak oft with thy Lord;
2. Take time to be ho - ly, The world rush-es on;
3. Take time to be ho - ly, Let Him be thy guide,
4. Take time to be ho - ly, Be calm in thy soul;

A - bide in Him al - ways, And feed on His word:
Spend much time in se - cret With Je - sus a - lone;
And run not be - fore Him What - ev - er be - tide;
Each tho't and each mo - tive Be - neath His con - trol;

Make friends of God's chil - dren, Help those who are weak;
By look - ing to Je - sus Like Him thou shalt be;
In joy or in sor - row Still fol - low thy Lord,
Thus led by His Spir - it To foun-tains of love,

For - get - ting in noth - ing His bless-ing to seek.
Thy friends in thy con - duct His like-ness shall see.
And look - ing to Je - sus, Still trust in His Word.
Thou soon shall be fit - ted For ser-vice a - bove. A - men.

O Master, Let Me Walk With Thee

Washington Gladden,
1836-1918

H. Percy Smith
1825-1898

1. O Master, let me walk with Thee In lowly paths of service free; Tell me Thy secret help me bear The strain of toil, the fret of care.

2. Help me the slow of heart to move By some clear, winning word of love; Teach me the wayward feet to stay, And guide them in the homeward way.

3. Teach me Thy patience; still with Thee In closer, dearer company, In work that keeps faith sweet and strong, In trust that triumphs over wrong.

4. In hope that sends a shining ray Far down the future's broad'ning way, In peace that only Thou canst give, With Thee, O Master, let me live. Amen.

Must Jesus Bear The Cross Alone?

Thomas Shepherd
1665-1739

George N. Allen
1812-1877

1. Must Je - sus bear the cross a - lone, And all the world go free? No, there's a cross for ev - 'ry - one, And there's a cross for me.

2. How hap - py are the saints a - bove, Who once went sor - rowing here! But they taste un - min - gled love, And joy with - out a tear.

3. The con - se - crat - ed cross I'll bear Till death shall set me free; And then go home my crown to wear, For there's a crown for me. A - men.

Come, Thou Fount

Robert Robinson
1735-1790

John Wyeth
1770-1858

1. Come, thou Fount of ev'ry bless - ing, Tune my heart to sing thy grace; Streams of
2. Here I raise mine Eb - e - ne - zer; High-er by thy help I'm come; And I
3. O to grace how great a debt - or Dai-ly I'm con-strained to be! Let thy

mer - cy, nev - er ceas - ing, Call for songs of loud - est praise, Teach me
hope, by thy good pleas - ure, Safe - ly To ar - rive at home. Je - sus
good - ness, like a fet - ter, Bind my wan - d'ring heart to thee: Prone to

some me - lo - dious son - net, sung by flam - ing tongues a - bove; Praise the
sought me when a stran - ger, Wan - d'ring from the fold of God; He, to
wan - der, Lord, I feel it, Prone to leave the God I love; Here's my

mount! I'm fixed up - on it, Mount of thy re - deem-ing love.
res - cue me from dan - ger, In - ter-posed his pre-cious blood.
heart, O take and seal it, Seal it for thy courts a - bove. A - men.

Breathe On Me, Breath Of God

Edwin Hatch
1835-1889

Robert Jackson
1842-1914

1. Breathe on me, Breath of God, Fill me with life a - new, That I may love what Thou dost love, And do what thou wouldst do.

2. Breathe on me, Breath of God, Un - till my heart is pure, Un - til with Thee I will one will, To do Glows with to en - dure.

3. Breathe on me, Breath of God, Till I am whol - ly Thine, Till all this earth - ly part of me Glows with Thy fire di - vine.

4. Breathe on me, Breath of God, So shall I nev - er die, But live with Thee the per - fect life Of Thine e - ter - ni - ty. A - men.

Stand Up, Stand Up For Jesus

George Duffield. Jr.
1818-1888

George J. Webb
1803-1887

1. Stand up, stand up for Je - sus, Ye sol - diers of the cross! Lift
2. Stand up, stand up for Je - sus, The trum - pet call o - bey; Forth
3. Stand up, stand up for Je - sus, Stand in His strength a - lone; The
4. Stand up, stand up for Je - sus, The strife will not be - long; This

high His roy - al ban — ner It must not suf - fer loss. From
to the might - y con - flict In this His glo - rious day. Ye
arm of flesh will fail you Ye dare not trust your own. Put
day the noise of bat - tle The next, the vic - tor's song. To

vic - t'ry un - to vic - t'ry His ar - my shall He lead,_____ Till
that are men now serve Him A - gainst un - num - bered foes'_____ Let
on the gos - pel ar - mor, Each piece put on with prayer;_____ Where
Him that o - ver - com - eth A crown of life shall be:_____ He

ev - 'ry foe is van - quished And Christ is Lord in - deed._____
cour - age rise with dan - ger And strength to strength op - pose._____
du - ty calls or dan - ger, Be nev - er want - ing there._____
with the King of glo - ry Shall reign e - ter - nal - ly._____ A - men.

Lead Us, O Father

William H. Burleigh
1812-1871

James Langran
1835-1909

1. Lead us, O Fa - ther, in the paths of peace:
2. Lead us, O Fa - ther, in the paths of truth:
3. Lead us, O Fa - ther, to Thy heav'n-ly rest,

With - out Thy guid - ing hand we go a - stray,
Un - helped by Thee, in er - ror's maze we grope,
How ev - er rough and steep the path may be,

And doubts ap - pall, and sor - rows still in - crease;
While pas - sion stains and fol - ly dims our youth,
Thru joy or sor - row, as Thou deem-est best,

Lead us thru Christ, the true and liv - ing Way.
And age comes on un-cheered by faith or hope.
Un - til our lives are per - fect - ed in Thee.

A - men.

Trust And Obey

John H. Sammis
1846-1919

Daniel B. Towner
1850-1919

1. When we walk with the Lord In the light of His Word, What a glo-ry He
2. Not a bur-den we bear, Not a sor-row we share, But our toil He doth
3. But we nev-er can prove The de-lights of His love Un-til all on the
4. Then in fel-low-ship sweet We will sit at His feet, Or we'll walk by His

sheds on our way! While we do His good will, He a-bides with us still, And with
rich-ly re-pay; Not a grief or a loss, Not a frown nor a cross, But is
al-tar we lay; For the fav-or He shows And the joy He be-stows Are for
side in the way; What He says we will do, Where He sends we will go; Nev-er

all who will trust and o-bey.
blest if we trust and o-bey.
them who will trust and o-bey.
fear, on-ly trust and o-bey.

Refrain

Trust and o-bey, for there's no oth-er

way To be hap-py in Je-sus, but to trust and o-bey. A-men.

Christ Be Beside Me

St. Patrick

Gaelic Melody

1. Christ be be - side me, Christ be be - fore me,
2. Christ on my right hand, Christ on my left hand,
3. Christ be in all hearts think - ing a - bout me;

Christ be be - hind me, King of my heart.
Christ all a - round me, shield in the strife.
Christ be on all tongues tell - ing of me.

Christ be with - in me, Christ be be - low me,
Christ in my sleep - ing, Christ in my sit - ting,
Christ be the vis - ion in eyes that see me;

Christ be a - bove me, nev - er to part.
Christ in my ris - ing, light of my life.
in ears that hear me, Christ ev-er - be.

65

Onward, Christian Soldiers

Sabine Baring-Gould
1834-1924

Arthur S. Sullivan
1842-1900

In Victory And Triumph We Sing

Bill Bay

Joyfully-Lively tempo

With the cross of Je - sus Go - ing on be - fore. A - men.

1. In vic - t'ry and tri - umph we sing; For our Sav - ior is Lord and King! God sent forth His Word like a bright, gleam - ing sword, And we stand on each prom - ise made.

2. In vic - t'ry and tri - umph we sing; To - tal heal - ing our Lord did bring! Je - sus cured sick and lame and His pow'r's just the same, So we call on that lov - ing name.

3. In vic - t'ry and tri - umph we sing; Our de - liv - 'rance He came to bring! Je - sus con - quered sin's pow'r and He saves us each hour As we call on that might - y name.

4. In vic - t'ry and tri - umph we sing; For Jes - us is Lord and King! God's Spir - it has come and our vic - t'ry is won, In His ar - my we're march - ing on.

Faith Of Our Fathers

Frederick W. Faber
1814-1863

Henri F. Hemy 1818-1888
Adapted by James
G. Walton 1821-1905

1. Faith of our fathers! living still In spite of dungeon,
2. Our fathers, chained in prisons dark, Were still in heart and
3. Faith of our fathers! faith and prayer Shall win all nations

fire, and sword: O how our hearts beat high with joy,
con - science free: And truly blest would be our fate,
on - to Thee; And thru the truth that comes from God,

When-e'er we hear that glo - rious word:
If we, like them, should die for Thee.
Man-kind shall then in - deed be free.

Refrain

Faith of our fa - thers,

ho - ly faith! We will be true to Thee till death. A - men.

Mine Eyes Have Seen The Glory

Julia Ward Howe

William Steffe

In The Cross Of Christ I Glory

John Bowring
1792-1872

Ithamar Conkey
1815-1867

1. In the cross of Christ I glory,
2. When the woes of life o'er take me,
3. When the sun of bliss is beam - ing
4. Bane and bless - ing, pain and plea - sure,

Tow - 'ring o'er the wrecks of time; All the
Hopes de - ceive, and fears an - noy, Nev - er
Light and love up - on my way, From the
By the cross are sanc - ti - fied; The peace is

light of sa - cred sto - ry Gath - ers
shall of the cross for sake me: Lo! it
cross the ra - diance stream - ing Adds more
there, that knows no mea - sure, Joys that

round its head sub - lime
glows with peace and joy.
lus - ter to the day.
thru all time a - bide.   A - men.

5. Repeat verse 1.

72

Jesus Shall Reign

Isaac Watts
1674-1748

John Hatton
1710-1793

1. Je - sus shall reign wher - e'er the sun
2. To Him shall end - less prayer be made,
3. Peo - ple and realms of ev - 'ry tongue
4. Let ev - 'ry crea - ture rise and bring

Does His suc - ces - sive jour - neys run;
And end - less prais - es crown His head;
Dwell on His love with sweet - est song,
His grate - ful hon - ors to our King;

His king - dom
His name like
And in - fant
An - gel de -

spread from shore to shore, Till moons shall
sweet per - fume shall rise With ev - 'ry
voic - es shall pro - claim Their ear - ly
scend with songs a - gain, And earth re -

wax and wane no more.
morn - ing sac - ri - fice.
bless - ings on His name!
peat the loud a - men!

A - men.

A Mighty Fortress Is Our God

Martin Luther
1483-1546

1. A might-y for-tress is our God A bul-wark nev-er fail - ing; Our
2. Did we in our own strength con-fide Our stri-ving would be los - ing, Were
3. And though this world, with dev-ils filled, Should threat-en to un-do us, We
4. That word a-bove all earth-ly pow'rs, No thanks to them, a-bid - eth; The

help - er He a mid the flood Of mor-tal ills pre-vail - ing: For
not the right man on our side, The man of God's own choos - ing: Dost
will not fear for God hath willed His truth to tri-umph through us. The
Spir - it and the gifts are ours Through Him who with us sid - eth: Let

still our an-cient foe, Doth seek to work us woe; His craft and pow'r are
ask who that may be? Christ Je-sus, it is He; Lord Sa-ba-oth, His
Prince of Dark-ness grim, We trem-ble not for him; His rage we can en-
goods and kin-dred go, This mor-tal life al-so; The bod-y they may

great, And armed with cru-el hate, On earth is not his e-qual.
name, From age to age the same, And He must win the bat-tle.
dure, For lo, his doom is sure; One lit-tle word shall fell him.
kill: God's truth a-bid-eth still; His king-dom is for-ev-er. A-men.

Majestic Sweetness Sits Enthroned

Samuel Stennett
1727-1795

Thomas Hastings
1784-1872

1. Ma - jes - tic sweet - ness sits en - throned Up -
2. No mor - tal can with Him com - pare A -
3. He saw me plunged in deep dis - tress And
4. To Him I owe my life and breath And

on the Sav - ior's brow; His head with ra - diant
mong the sons of men; Fair - er is He than
flew to my re - lief; For me He bore the
all the joys I have; He makes me tri - umph

glo - ries crowned, His lips with grace o'er - flow, His
all the fair Who fill the heav'n - ly train, Who
shame - ful cross And car - ried all my grief, And
o - ver death And saves me from the grave, And

lips with grace o'er - flow.
fill the heav'n - ly train.
car - ried all my grief.
saves me from the grave.

A - men.

75

Rejoice The Lord Is King

Charles Wesley
1707-1788

John Darwall
1731-1789

1. Re - joice, the Lord is King: Your Lord and King a - dore! Re -
2. Je - sus, the Sav - ior, reigns, The God of truth and love; When
3. His king - dom can - not fail, He rules o'er earth and heav'n; The

joice, give thanks and sing, And tri - umph ev - er - more: Lift
He had purged our stains, He took His seat a - bove: He
keys of death and hell Are to our Je - sus giv'n:

up your heart, lift up your voice! Re -

joice, a - gain I say, re - joice! A - men.

My Faith Looks Up To Thee

Ray Palmer
1808-1887

Lowell Mason
1792-1872

O Zion, Haste

Mary A. Thompson
1834-1923

James Walch
1837-1901

1. O Zi - on haste, thy mis-sion high ful - fill - ing, To tell to
2. Be - hold how man - y thou-sands still are ly - ing Bound in the
3. Pro - claim to ev - 'ry peo-ple, tongue and na - tion That God in
4. Give of thy sons to bear the mes - sage glo - rious Give of thy

all the world that God is Light, That He who
dark — some pris - on house of sin, With none to
whom they live and move is Love: Tell how He
wealth to speed them on their way; Pour out thy

made all na - tions is not will - ing One soul should
tell them of the Sav - ior's dy - ing Or of the
stooped to save His last cre - a - tion And died on
soul for them in pray'r vic - to - rious, And all thou

per - ish, lost in shades of night.
life He died for them to win.
earth that man might live a - bove.
spend - est Je - sus will re - pay.

Refrain

Pub - lish glad

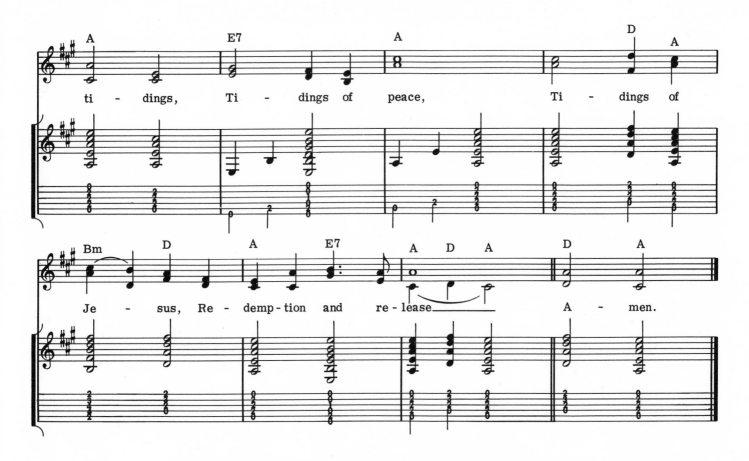

The Lord Is My Shepherd

Jessie Seymour Irving
1836-1887

From the Scottish
Psalter, 1650

1. The Lord's my Shep - herd I'll not want; He makes me down to lie In
2. My soul he doth re - store a - gain, And me to walk doth make With-
3. Yea, tho' I walk thru death's dark vale, Yet will I fear no ill, For

pas - tures green He lead - eth me The Qui - et wa - ters by.
in the paths of right - eous - ness, E'en for His own name's sake.
Thou art with me, and Thy rod And staff me com - fort still.

E F#m G#m F#m E B7 E   B   F#7   B7   E F#m G#m F#m E B7 E   B   F#7 B7
4. My table Thou hast furnished In presence of my foes;   5. Goodness and mercy all my life shall surely follow me,

E   AE   B7 E AEAE   F#m   E B7 E   E   AE   B7   EAEAE   F#m   E B7 E
My head Thou dost with oil anoint, And my cup overflows .   And in God's house forevermore My dwelling place shall be.

79

Lead On, O King Eternal

Ernest Shurtleff
1862-1917

Henry Smart
1813-1879

1. Lead on, O King e - ter - nal, The day of march has come; Hence-
2. Lead on, O King e - ter - nal, Till sin's fierce war shall cease, And
3. Lead on, O King e - ter - nal, We fol - low, not with fears, For

forth in fields of con - quest Thy tents shall be our home. Through
ho - li - ness shall whis - per The sweet a - men of peace. For
glad - ness breaks like morn - ing Wher - e'er Thy face ap - pears. Thy

days of prep - a - ra - tion Thy grace has made us strong, And
not with swords loud clash - ing, Nor roll of stir - ring drums, With
cross is lift - ed o'er us; We jour - ney in its light; The

now, O King e - ter - nal, We lift our bat - tle song.
deeds of love and mer - cy, The heav'n - ly king - dom comes
crown a - waits the con - quest; Lead on, O God of might. A - men.

I Sing The Mighty Power Of God

Isaac Watts
1674-1748

From Gesangbuch der Herzogl,
Württemberg, 1784

1. I sing the might-y pow'r of God That made the moun-tains rise, That spread the flow-ing seas a-broad And built the loft-y skies. I sing the wis-dom that or-dained The sun to rule the day; The moon shines full at His com-mand, And all the stars o-bey.

2. I sing the good-ness of the Lord That filled the earth with food; He formed the crea-tures with His word And then pro-nounced them good. Lord, how Thy won-ders are dis-played Where-e'er I turn my eye; If I sur-vey the ground I tread Or gaze up-on the sky!

3. There's not a plant or flow'r be-low But makes Thy glo-ries known; And clouds a-rise and tem-pests blow By or-der from Thy throne; While all that bor-rows life from Thee Is ev-er in Thy care, And ev-'ry-where that man can be, Thou, God, art pres-ent there. A-men.

God Of Our Fathers

Daniel C. Roberts
1841-1907

George W. Warren
1828-1902

1. God of our fa - thers, whose al might - y hand.
2. Thy love di - vine hath led us in the past;
3. From war's a - larms, from dead - ly pes - ti - lence,

Leads forth in beau - ty all the star - ry band
In this free land by Thee our lot is cast;
Be Thy strong arm our ev - er sure de - fense;

Of shin - ing
Be Thou our
Thy true re -

Worlds in splen - der thru the skies,
rul - er, guard - ian, guide, and stay,
li - gion in our hearts in - crease,

Our grate - ful
Thy Word our
Thy boun - teous

Songs be - fore Thy throne a - rise.
law, Thy paths our cho - sen way.
good - ness nour - ish us in peace.

A - men.

O God, Our Help In Ages Past

5. O God, our help in ages past, Our hope for years to come, Be Thou our guide while life shall last, And our eternal home.

Come, Thou Long Expected Jesus

Charles Wesley
1707-1788

Rowland H. Prichard
1811-1877

1. Come, Thou long ex - pect - ed Je - sus, Born to set Thy peo - ple
2. Born Thy peo - ple to de - liv - er, Born a child and yet a

free; From our fears and sins re - lease us; Let us find our
King, Born to reign in us for - ev - er, Now Thy gra - cious

rest in Thee. Is - rael's strength and con - so - la - tion, Hope of
king - dom bring. By Thine own e - ter - nal Spir - it Rule in

all the earth Thou art; Dear de - sire of ev - 'ry na - tion,
all our hearts a - lone; By Thine all suf - fi - cient mer - it,

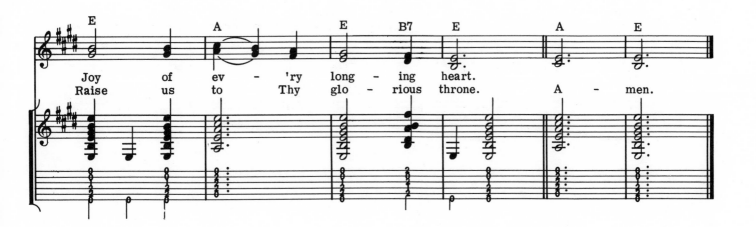

Joy of ev - 'ry long - ing heart.
Raise us to Thy glo - rious throne. A - men.

Alleluia, Sing To Jesus

1. Alleluia! sing to Jesus! His the scepter, His the throne;
   Alleluia! His the triumph, His the victory alone;
   Hark! the songs of peaceful Zion thunder like a mighty flood;
   Jesus out of every nation hath redeemed us by His blood.

2. Alleluia! not as orphans are we left in sorrow now;
   Alleluia! He is near us, Faith believes, nor questions how:
   Though the cloud from sight received Him when the forty days were o'er,
   Shall our hearts forget His promise, "I am with you evermore"?

3. Alleluia! Bread of Heaven, Thou on earth our food, our stay!
   Alleluia! here the sinful flee to Thee from day to day;
   Intercessor, friend of sinners, earth's Redeemer, plead for me;
   Where the songs of all the sinless sweep across the crystal sea.

Peace I Give You

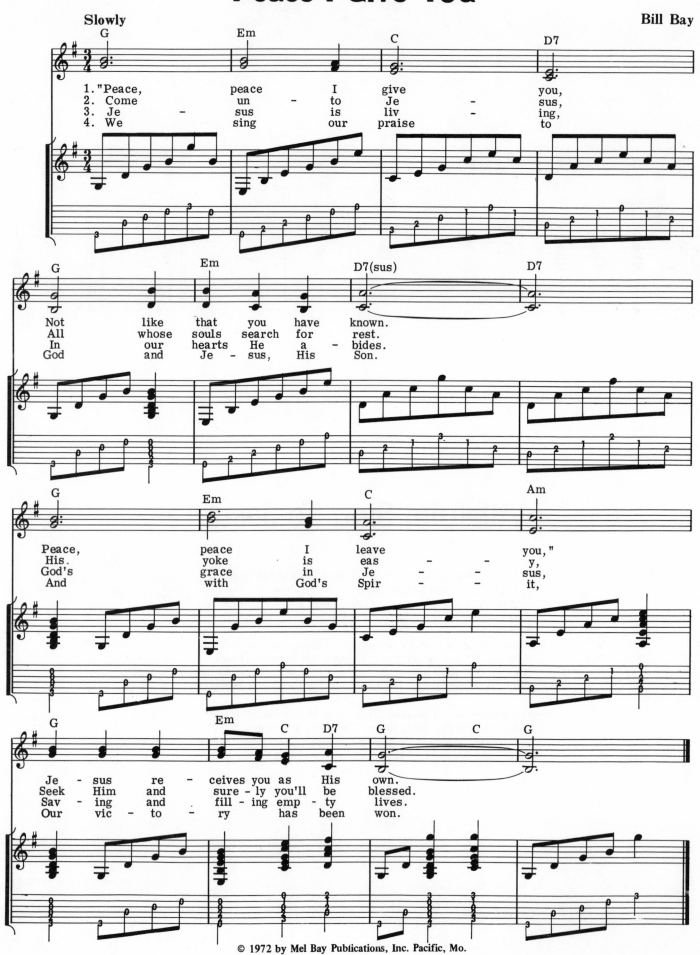

Nearer, My God, To Thee

Sarah F. Adams
1805-1848

Lowell Mason
1792-1872

1. Near - er, my God to Thee, Near - er to Thee! E'en tho it be a-cross That rais - eth me, Still all my song shall be, Near - er, my God, to Thee; Near - er my God, to Thee, Near - er to Thee!

2. There let the way ap-pear, Steps un - to heav'n; All that Thou send - est me, In mer - cy giv'n; An - gels to beck - on me Near - er, my God, to Thee; Near - er my God, to Thee, Near - er to Thee!

3. Then, with my wak - ing thoughts Bright - with Thy praise, Out of my ston - y griefs Beth - el I'll raise; So by my woes to be Near - er, my God, to Thee; Near - er my God, to Thee; Near - er to Thee!

4. Or if on joy - ful wing Cleav - ing the sky, Sun, moon, and stars for-got, Up - ward I fly, Still all my song shall be, Near - er, my God, to Thee; Near - er my God, to Thee; Near - er to Thee! A - men.

The Church's One Foundation

Samuel J. Stone
1839-1900

Samuel S. Wesley
1820-1876

1. The Church's one foun-da-tion Is Je-sus Christ her Lord; She is His new cre-a-tion By wa-ter and the word. From heav'n He came and sought her To be His ho-ly bride; With His own blood He bought her, And for her life He died.

2. E-lect from ev-'ry na-tion, Yet one o'er all the earth, Her char-ter of sal-va-tion, One Lord, one faith, one birth; One ho-ly name she bless-es, Par-takes one ho-ly food, And To one hope she press-es, With ev-'ry grace en-dued.

3. Yet she on earth hath un-ion With God the three in One, And mys-tic sweet com-mu-nion With those whose rest is won. O hap-py ones and ho-ly! Lord, give us grace that we, Like them, the meek and low-ly, On high may dwell with thee. A-men.

On Jordan's Stormy Banks

Samuel Stennett
1727-1795

Amerian Folk Melody

1. On Jor-dan's storm-y banks I stand, And cast a wish-ful eye To
2. O'er all those wide ex-tend-ed plains Shines one e-ter-nal day; There
3. When I shall reach that hap-py place, I'll be for-ev-er blest, For

Ca-naan's fair and hap-py land, Where my pos-ses-sions lie, O
God the Son for-ev-er-reigns, And scat-ters night a-way. No
I shall see my Fa-ther's face, And in his bos-om rest. Filled

the trans-port-ing rap-turous scene That ris-es to my sight: Sweet
chill-ing winds of poi-sonous breath Can reach that health-ful shore; Sick-
with de-light my rap-tured soul Lives out its earth-ly day; And

fields ar-rayed in liv-ing green And riv-ers of de-light!
ness and sor-row, pain and death, Are falt and feared no more.
then, though Jor-dan's waves may roll, I'll fear-less launch a-way   A-men.

89

Oh God, We Praise Thee

Laud, C.M.

Wyeth's Repository of Sacred Music Part Second, 1813

1. O God! we praise Thee, and con-fess That Thou the on-ly Lord; And
2. To Thee all an-gels cry a-loud; To Thee the pow'rs on high, Both
3. O ho-ly, ho-ly, ho-ly Lord, Whom heav'n-ly hosts o-bey, The
4. The ho-ly, church through out the world, O Lord, con-fess-es Thee, That

ev-er-last-ing Fa-ther art, By all the earth a-dored.
cher-u-bim and ser-a-phim Con-tin-ual-ly do cry.
world is with the glo-ry filled Of Thy ma-jes-tic sway!
Thou e-ter-nal Fa-ther art, Of bound-less ma-jes-ty!

I Will Arise And Go To Jesus

Joseph Hart
1712-1768

Note-Sing verse 1 after each other verse

Southern Folk Melody

1. I will a-rise and go to Je-sus, He will em-brace me in His arms;
2. Come, ye sin-ners, poor and need-y, Weak and wound-ed, sick and sore;
3. Come, ye thirst-y, come, and wel-come, God's free boun-ty glo-ri-fy;

In the arms of my dear Sav-ior, Oh, there are ten thou-sand charms.
Je-sus read-y stands to save you, Full of pit-y, love, and pow'r.
True be-lief and true re-pent-ance, Ev-'ry grace that brings you nigh. A-men.

Come, Ye Disconsolate

Thomas Moore, 1779-1852
Alt. by Thomas Hastings,
1784-1872

From a collection of Motets
or Antiphons, London, 1792
Samuel Webbe, Sr.
1740-1816

1. Come, ye dis - con - so-late, wher - e'er ye lan - guish, Come to the
2. Joy of the des - o-late, light of the stray - ing, Hope of the
3. Here see the Bread of Life; see wa - ters flow - ing Forth from the

mer - cy seat, fer - vent - ly kneel; Here bring your
pen - i - tent, fade - less and pure! Here speaks the
throne of God, pure from a - bove: Come to the

wound - ed hearts, here tell your an - guish: Earth has no
Com — for-ter, ten - der - ly say - ing, Earth has no
feast of love; come, ev - er know - ing Earth has no

sor - row that heav'n can - not heal.
sor - row that heav'n can - not cure."
sor - row that heav'n can - not move. A - men.

My Faith Has Found A Resting Place

Lidie H. Edmunds 19th Cent.

Norwegian Melody

1. My faith has found a rest-ing place Not in de-vice nor creed: I
2. My heart is lean-ing on the Word The writ-ten Word of God: Sal-
3. My great Phy-si-cian heals the sick, The lost He came to save; For

trust the Ev-er-liv-ing One His wounds for me shall plead.
va-tion by my Sav-ior's name Sal-va-tion thru His blood. I
me His pre-cious blood He shed, For me His life He gave.

need no oth-er ar-gu ment, I need no oth-er plea; It

is e-nough that Je-sus died, And that He died for me. A-men.

Begin, My Tongue, Some Heavenly Theme

Isaac Watts
1674-1748

From Henny W.
Greatorex's Collection,
1851

1. Be - gin, my tongue, some heav'n - ly theme, And
2. Tell of His won - drous faith - ful - ness, And
3. His ver - y word of grace is strong, As
4. Oh, might I hear Thy heav'n - ly tongue But

speak some bound - less thing; The might - y
sound His pow'r a - broad; Sing the sweet
that which built the sky; The voice that
whis - per, "Thou art mine!" Those gen - tle

works or might - ier name Of our e -
prom - ise of His grace And the per -
rolls the stars a - long Pro - claims it
words should raise my song To notes al -

ter - nal King.
for - ming God.
from on high. A - men.
most di - vine.

I Need Thee Every Hour

Annie S. Hawks
1835-1918

Robert Lowry
1826-1899

1. I need Thee ev-'ry hour, Most gra - cious Lord; No
2. I need Thee ev-'ry hour, Stay Thou near by; Temp -
3. I need Thee ev-'ry hour, In joy or pain; Come
4. I need Thee ev-'ry hour, Most Ho - ly one; O

ten - der voice like Thine Can peace af - ford.
ta - tions lose their pow'r When thou art nigh
quick - ly and a - bide, Or life is vain.
make me Thine in - deed, Thou bless - ed Son.

Chorus

I need Thee O I need Thee, Ev - 'ry hour I need Thee, O bless me now, my

Sav - ior I come to Thee! A - men.

Now The Day Is Over

Sabine Baring-Gould
1834-1924

Joseph Barnby
1838-1896

1. Now the day is o – ver, Night is draw – ing
2. Je – sus, give the wea – ry Calm and sweet re –
3. Grant to lit – tle child – ren Vi – sions bright of

nigh; Shad – ows of the eve – ning
pose; With thy ten – derest bless – ing
Thee; Guard the sail – ors toss – ing

steal a – cross the sky.
may our eye – lids close.
on the deep, blue sea. A – men.

C G C
4. Through the long night watches,
Am E7 Am
May thine angels spread
D7   G C
Their white wings above me,
G G7 C
Watching round my bed.

C G C
5. When the morning wakens,
Am E7 Am
Then may I arise
D7   G C
Pure and fresh and sinless
G G7 C
In Thy holy eyes.

Wondrous Love

Southern Harmony, 1835

How Firm A Foundation

"K" in Rippon's Selection
of Hymns, 1787

Early American Melody
from "Union Harmony"
1837

1. How firm a foun - da - tion, ye saints of the Lord, Is
2. "Fear not I am with thee O be not dis - mayed, For
3. "When thru the deep wa - ters I call thee to go, The
4. "When thru fi - ery tri - als thy path - way shall lie. My

laid for your faith in His ex - cel - lent Word! What
I am thy God, I will still give thee aid; I'll
riv - ers of woe shall not thee o - ver flow; For
grace, all suf - fi - cient, shall be thy sup - ply; The

more can He say than to you He hath said To
strength - en thee, help thee, and cause thee to stand, Up -
I will be with thee thy trou - bles to bless, And
flame shall not hurt thee I on - ly de - sign Thy

you, who for ref - uge to Je - sus have fled?
held by my gra - cious, om - nip - o - tent hand."
sanc - ti - fy to thee thy deep - est dis - tress."
dross to con - sume and thy gold to re - fine." A - men.

5. "The soul that on Jesus hath leaned for repose, I will not, I will not desert to his foes;
That soul, tho all hell should endeavor to shake, I'll never, no, never, no, never forsake!"

Abide With Me

Henry Lyte
1793-1847

Wm. H. Monk
1823-1889

1. A - bide with me; fast falls the e - ven - tide;
2. Swift to its close ebbs out life's lit - tle day;
3. I need thy pres - ence ev - 'ry pass - ing hour;
4. Hold Thou Thy cross be - fore my clos - ing eyes;

The dark - ness deep - ens; its Lord, with me a - bide!
Earth's joys grow dim; its glo - ries pass a - way;
What but Thy grace can foil the temp - ter's pow'r?
Shine through the gloom, and point me to the skies:

When oth - er help - ers fail and com - forts flee,
Change and de - cay in all a - round I see;
Who, like Thy - self, my guide and stay can be?
Heav'n's mor - ning breaks and earth's vain shad - ows flee:

Help of the help - less, O a - bide with me.
O Thou who chang - est not, a - bide with me.
Through cold and sun - shine, O a - bide with me.
In life, in death, O Lord, a - bide with me. A - men.

What A Friend We Have In Jesus

Joseph Scriven
1832-1918

Charles C. Converse
1819-1886

1. What a friend we have in Je - sus All our sins and griefs to bear!
2. Have we trials - and temp - ta - tions? Is there trouble an - y - where?
3. Are we weak and heav-y la - den, Cum - bered with a load of care?

What a priv - i - lege to car - ry ev - 'ry-thing to God in prayer!
We should nev-er be dis-cour - aged, Take it to the Lord in prayer!
Pre - cious Sa-vior, still our re - fuge, Take it to the Lord in prayer!

O what peace we of - ten for - feit, O what need-less pain we bear,
Can we find a friend so faith - ful Who will all our sor-rows share?
Do thy friends de-spise, for sake thee? Take it to the Lord in prayer,

All be-cause we do not car - ry Ev - 'ry-thing to Good in prayer!
Je - sus knows our ev -'ry weak - ness Take it to the Lord in prayer!
In His arms He'll take and shield thee, Thou wilt find a sol-ace there. A - men.

Rock Of Ages

Augustus M. Toplady
1740-1778

Thomas Hastings
1784-1872

1. Rock of A - ges, cleft for me, Let me
2. Could my tears for - ev - er flow, Could my
3. While I draw this fleet - ing breath, When my

hide my - self in thee', Let the wa - ter and the blood, From Thy
zeal no lan - guor know, These for sin could not a - tone; Thou must
eyes shall close in death, When I rise to worlds un - known, And be -

wound - ed side which flowed, Be of sin the dou - ble
save, and Thou a - lone. In my hand no price I
hold Thee on Thy throne, Rock of A - ges, cleft for

cure Save from wrath and make me pure.
bring; Sim - ply to Thy cross I cling.
me, Let me hide my - self in Thee. A - men.

This Is My Father's World

Maltbie O.Babcock
1858-1901

Franklin L.Sheppard
1852-1930

Blest Be The Tie That Binds

John Fawcett
1740-1817

alt B7 form used 2nd fret

Johann G. Naegeli
1773-1836

1. Blest be the tie that binds Our
2. Be - fore our Fa - ther's throne We
3. We share each oth - er's woes Our
4. When we a - sun - der part, It

hearts in Chris - tian love: The fel - low
pour our ar - dent prayers; Our fear, our
mu - tual bur - dens bear, And of - ten
gives us in - ward pain; But we shall

ship of kin - dred minds Is like to
hopes, our aims are one, Our com - forts
for each oth - er flows The sym - pa -
still be joined in heart, And hope to

that a - bove.
and our cares.
thiz - ing tear.
meet a - gain. A - men.

How Heavenly Is The Sight
(1 John 4:21)

J. Swain   W. Bay

5. Love is the golden chain that binds The happy souls above; And he's an heir of heaven who finds His heart a glow with love.

Ancient Of Days

William L. Doane
1832-1913

J. Albert Jeffery,
1854-1929

1. Ancient of days, who sittest throned in glory, To Thee all knees are
2. O holy Father, who hast led Thy children In all the ages
3. O holy Jesus, Prince of Peace and Savior, To Thee we owe the

bent all voices pray; Thy love has blessed the wide world's wondrous story
with the fire and cloud, Thru seas dry-shod, thru weary wastes bewild'ring,
peace that still prevails, Stilling the rude wills of men's wild behavior,

With light and life since Eden's dawning day.
To Thee in rev-'rent love our hearts are bowed.
And calming passion's fierce and stormy gales. Amen.

```
        C           F    C     G       F  G
4. O Holy Ghost, the Lord and the Life giver,
     C    Am   G    C   G       D7      G
   Thine is the quickening pow'r that gives increase:
     Am        Dm        Am       Dm Am
   From Thee have flowed, as from a mighty river,
     C                  G   G7  C
   Our faith and hope, our fellowship and peace.
```

```
        C           F    C     G     F  G
5. O Triune God, with heart and voice adoring,
     C    Am   G    C   G       D7      G
   Praise we the goodness that doth crown our days;
     Am        Dm        Am       Dm Am
   Pray we that Thou wilt hear us, still imploring
     C                 G  G7  C
   Thy love and favor, kept to us always.
```

Were You There

Spiritual

1. Were you there when they cru - ci - fied my Lord?_____ Were you
2. Were you there when they nailed Him to the tree?_____ Were you
3. Were you there when they laid Him in the tomb?_____ Were you

there when they cru - ci - fied my Lord?_____
there when they nailed Him to the tree?_____
there when they laid Him in the tomb?_____ Oh!_____

Some-times it caus - es me to trem-ble, trem-ble,

trem-ble._____ Were you there when they cru - ci - fied my Lord?_____
Were you there when they nailed Him to the tree?_____
Were you there when they laid Him in the tomb?_____ A - men.

Gethsemane, Destiny!

(Based On Matthew 26)

Bill Bay

O Sacred Head, Now Wounded

Attr. To Bernard of Clairvaux 1091-1153
Trans. by Paul Gerhandt 1607-1676 (German)
Trans. by James Alexander 1804-1859 (English)

Hans Leo Hassler
1564-1612

1. O sa-cred Head, now wound-ed, With grief and shame weighed down, Now
2. What Thou, my Lord, hast suf-fered Was all for sin-ners' gain; Mine,
3. What lan-guage shall I bor-row To thank Thee, dear-est friend, For

scorn-ful-ly sur-round-ed With thorns, thine on-ly crown: How
mine was the trans-gres-sion, But Thine the dead-ly pain. Lo,
this Thy dy-ing sor-row, Thy pit-y with-out end? O

pale Thou art with an—guish, With sore a-buse and scorn! How
here I fall, my Sav—ior! 'Tis I de-serve Thy place; Look
Make me Thine for-ev—er; And should I faint-ing be Lord,

does that vis-age lan—guish Which once was bright as morn!
on me with Thy fa—vor, Vouch-safe to me Thy grace.
let me nev-er, ne—ver Out live my love to Thee. A—men.

107

Christ The Lord Is Risen Today

Charles Wesley and others
1707-1788

Altered 1749 from
Lyradavidica, 1708

1. Christ the Lord is ris'n to-day,
2. Lives a-gain our glo-rious King,
3. Loves re-deem-ing work is done,
4. Soar we now where Christ has led,

Al - le - lu - ia!

Sons of men and an-gels say,
Where, O death, is now thy sting?
Fought the fight, the bat-tle won,
Fo-l'wing our ex-halt-ed Head,

Al - le - lu - ia!

Raise your joys and tri-umphs high,
Once He died our souls to save,
Death in vain for-bids Him rise,
Made like Him, like Him we rise,

Al - le - lu - ia!

Sing, ye heav'ns and earth re-ply,
Where's thy vic-to-ry O grave?
Christ hath o-pened par-a-dise,
Ours the cross, the grave the skies,

Al - le - lu - ia!

A - men.

The Strife Is Over

Latin Hymn
Trans. by Francis Pott

G. P. Sante Da Palestrina
1525-1594
Adapted by W. H. Monk
1823-1889

Christ Arose

Robert Lowry
1826-1899

1. Low in the grave He lay, Je - sus my Sav - ior! Wait - ing the
2. Vain - ly they watch His bed, Je - sus my Sav - ior! Vain - ly they
3. Death can - not keep his prey, Je - sus my Sav - ior! He tore the

com - ing day,
seal the dead Je - sus my Lord! Up from the grave He a-
bars a - way,

rose, With a might-y tri-umph o'er His foes; He a-rose a vic-tor from the

dark do - main, And He lives for - ev - er with His saints to reign. He a-

Praise, My Soul, The King Of Heaven

Henry F. Lyte
1793-1847

Henry Smart
1813-1879

1. Praise, my soul, the King of heav-en, To His feet thy tri-bute bring;
2. Praise Him for His grace and fa-vor To our fa-thers in dis-tress;
3. Fath-er-like, He tends and spares us; Well our fee-ble frame He knows;
4. An-gels in the height; a-dore Him; Ye be-hold Him face to face;

Ran-somed, healed, re-stored, for-giv-en, Ev-er-more His prais-es sing.
Praise Him, still the same as ev-er, Slow to chide, and swift to bless.
In His hands He gent-ly bears us, Res-cues us from all our foes.
Saints tri-umph-ant bow be-fore Him Gath-ered in from ev-'ry race.

Al-le-lu-ia! Al-le-lu-ia! Praise the ev-er-last-ing King.
Al-le-lu-ia! Al-le-lu-ia! Glo-rious in His faith-ful-ness.
Al-le-lu-ia! Al-le-lu-ia! Wide-ly yet His mer-cy flows.
Al-le-lu-ia! Al-le-lu-ia! Praise with us the God of grace. A-men.

Lord Dismiss Us With Thy Blessing
(Sicilian Mariners)

John Fawcett,
1740-1817

From Tattersall's
"Psalmody" 1794